To Ryan ~

with gratitude
for his friendship
+
admiration for his work,

Blue Norther and Other Poems

Bedford Clark

7/11/16

Blue Norther
and Other Poems

William Bedford Clark (signature)

William Bedford Clark

Texas Review Press
Huntsville, Texas

FIRST EDITION, 2010
Requests for permission to reproduce material from this work should be sent to:

> Permissions
> Texas Review Press
> English Department
> Sam Houston State University
> Huntsville, TX 77341-2146

Acknowledgements:

A number of these poems, sometimes in slightly different form, originally appeared in the following journals and anthologies: *Academic Questions, Christianity and Literature, Francis and Clare in Poetry, Grasslands Review, Homage to RPW, Louisiana English Journal, Modern Age, New Texas, Place of Passage, Points of Gold, Sewanee Review, Shawagunk Review, South Carolina Review, Southern Review, Southwestern American Literature, Windhover, Xavier Review.*

Cover photo: William Kim McPherson, "Street Scene: Gene Autry, Oklahoma, c. 1967" (used by permission).

Author photo: Eleanor Clark Barton

Library of Congress Cataloging-in-Publication Data

Clark, William Bedford.
  Blue norther and other poems / William Bedford Clark. -- 1st ed.
      p. cm.
  ISBN-13: 978-1-933896-43-4 (pbk. : alk. paper)
  ISBN-10: 1-933896-43-4 (pbk. : alk. paper)
  1. Southwestern States--Poetry. I. Title.
  PS3603.L3696B58 2010
  811'.6--dc22

                                        2010005075

In Memoriam

Andrew Garay
(1926-2005)

&

Luis Costa
(1942-2006)

Contents

Fearsome as the skull of a six-horned ram,
Wide-socketed, with fissured grin,
Is the deep itch of disremembered May
That scorns the now, invents a then.

Blue Norther

Last night, frost broke the earth's back,
And the earth turned in upon itself again.
The norther, blue, swift, and merciless,
Caught vine and wren, late rose and gecko unprepared.

The tortoise on hard ground must freeze.
Squirrels will try their teeth on his empty shell.

Now you may walk the ominous backlot
With impunity. No scorpion, spider, no brown wasp
Will challenge your tenuous hegemony.
Their green world has turned gray.

Today the mistletoe is made manifest.
It has waited for its time against the sky.

These are the first signs of a darkling season.
A few stunned leaves still cling to the tree.
You can do nothing. Build a fire.
Break out the chili pot. Pour a tall whiskey.

Like wren or vine, gecko or late rose,
You are unprepared.

Suburbia could use its Hesiod,
Its Virgil or Horace.
We have need of old wisdom,
Here along Burton Creek.

Sketch in Charcoal

The day is gray with cold
    that creeps into the culvert cracks
    and shames the sun into hiding
Beyond fields where fenceposts cast no shadows.

Behind the dingy shuttered pane
    the attic dust is frozen
    like time to a tainted daguerreotype
    or lovers' songs to cylinders of brittle wax
Beside the needleless victrola.

Below
    the old man has grown too deaf to know
    whose ghost whispers on the stairs.

Plains Song

The Kiowas, Comanches, the crafty Osage
Knew these places, but passed them by
Downwind, so as to leave no trail on the sharp air,
For *little folk* liked slow creeks, maimed timber.

Having less sense, we built stony houses, broad lawns,
Saved oaks, sank ponds, named these places.
The gushers spewed new greasy wealth, golf-courses
     greened,
But the dry wind keened in the mind's deep ear.

Even when the oil came at us third-hand, slick, black,
But sure, we settled on tight lots
Where trees were dwarfs, the new moon failed, things
     disappeared,
And the quick wind raised strange notions by night.

Trust the trees.

They have a thing to say.

There are those places that are bad beyond reason.

Turn the horses downwind.

Lawncare

The duststorm's black wall in mid-afternoon
Was a sign in our fathers' time that soon
The thick wind would hurl back what was taken
By slow tractors and rutting plow. Shaken
From the tough roots of prairie grass, the soil
Had turned to fine silt under August's glowing coil.

Now grackles do their quick Jurassic strut
And bob and jog behind my mower. I cut
The bristling grass of late August and small
Pale crickets are dispossessed. Almost all
Are claimed by a precise surgical beak.
(The coughing motor drowns out any clack or squeak.)

It may be grass is best left to itself,
Like Depression glass on a what-not shelf.

Tenure Deliberations

Today the dossiers sit at the head
Of the long table where the Chair convenes
Our meeting. *What we say must not be said
Outside this room.* We adopt this strict means
Against litigation. Bile and rumor
Move among us as silent witnesses,
While we debate journals, imprints, ardor
In the classroom, what a reviewer says.

Six years, up or out! Nothing personal . . .
But the grim stakes are higher still, for we
Are in the dock; each candidate's record
Serves as rebuke or vindication. All
Here must judge themselves too and secretly
Cower in what peace tenure may afford.

Sinphonia

The devil's voice like muted brass suggests
A theme soon taken up and subjected
To clever modulations. Bird's-eye rests
Quicken the ear to notes undeflected
(No, amplified) by the troubled quiet:

You can hold your gin. Your wife could diet,
And should. The slim bright girl in the third row
May be a Mormon, but squirms to be yours.
Can a man's reputation ever grow
With three classes? Your new colleagues are boors.

The tune is predictable, which is its
Appeal, for there's little time to listen
With much discernment. Still, the muted pitch
Is a bit too low, the phrasing brazen.

For RB

(with whatever apologies may be due)

Always a joker, time comes across kind,
And the old poet's gush of white bright hair
Promises much—more than his words will bear
By reading's end. He breaks each vatic line
With *sotto voce* growls against the war,
Right-wing flagmen, America the whore.

Off to one side, a barefoot, boyish man
Declines on a low hard bench, teasing riffs
From—no lie—a tall sitar. Music drifts . . .
A ghostly peacock's pale denuded fan.
The poet implies we'd do well to shoot
Every oil-pimping son at Brown & Root.

The sitar preens beneath the nasal rant.
You'd like to leave; decorum says you can't.

Demographics

My Texas town is filled with lean philosophers
Who give the University the widest berth
They can, and wisely so. They feel the straining earth
Wheeze *Sein und Zeit* as day goes down, know work confers
No automatic dignity. The Mexican
On the child's bike who pumps his angling way toward home
(A peeled duplex) anticipates the shower and comb
That will affirm the baptized grace of errant man.

We worry at a tissue of signifiers,
And deconstruct the Holocaust as social text:
Juan Ramos caught his finger in some stubborn pliers
And cursed—will send real money home on Friday next.

Welcome Northeast High Class of '65

It does look toward the great Resurrection,
Bodies transformed if hardly transfigured:
Crow's feet, bald knobs, cheerleaders now broad-reared,
Most guys fretting a swollen midsection
Like pregnant girls who couldn't graduate
On time. We punch memory files for names
And speak of cars, dead teachers, hardwon games,
Childbirths, divorce. Having reached fifty-eight,
We drop old distinctions, are finally
Diplomaed members of a single class
Who've learned how pride is always slippery
While shame is sure. May this new lesson last.

But note how the plainest girl is grown elegant,
And every bullied dunce has proved intelligent.

Oklahoma City

No one that I knew that I know of died.
But many who used to swim at Springlake,
Then ride the Big Dipper, toss for a cake,
Or play the Arcade while their swimsuits dried
Were hit where they loved at the hub of spring.
A blast is a sudden, impartial thing.

We'd trained for tornadoes from grade-school on;
Dived under desks; covered our heads. Each noon
On Saturday a siren moaned, but soon
We learned it was "only a test" (and gone
Before long the barbed fear that snagged your breath).
We traded jokes against ballistic death.

What you expect don't come, Aunt Ruby said.
She got it right. Disaster is the guest
Who doesn't knock and catches you at rest—
A rented truck, piled rubble splacked with red,
Prefer a morning at the hub of spring.
A bomb is a sudden, impartial thing.

Old Carmichael

(Scene: The Oklahoma City Zoo, c. 1956)

Emphatic, tapered like a concert grand,
The Arctic bear, not now quite white,
Ivory'd by age or carbon-drift, began
His roll-shoulder stroll. Swinging right,
He'd lift his nose (black too, those clawsome paws!)
Into each corner of his cage—
A quick step back, a slight strategic pause:
A tired old hoofer dragged onstage.

Day after day, from noon to leaning dark,
He paced the same precise box-trot
In a twelve-by-twelve pen in Lincoln Park.
Some ursine Zen retreat from thought?
Perhaps. We children watched with nascent guilt,
But glad for double rows of bars, a cube well-built.

Otto Hinckelmann, Pianist

Otto, you were my teacher's friend, and you,
Like all refugees, had a story we
Knew was too total to count only true
Of you alone. That is shared history.

There was the terror in stark green, then red—
The loss of *gelt*, then self. Turn it around
And the equation is no better said:
One woman's scream another's coital sound.

What of the pale Czech girl's wet, tonguey kiss?
What of the Russian rifle's focused stare?
What of slow Schumann played before a tryst?
The smell of flames and dust displacing air?

You outlived bliss and dread, old Otto, friend.
I didn't come to see you at the end.

Cultural History

At thirteen, the Sixties began for him
When he watched Sue tuck her ponytail up
Under itself to make a neat, full cup
Of off-blond hair. She was the sister Jim,
His friend, said smoked and let herself be felt,
So he went warm and wet below the belt.

Boys will be men, and some, like Jim, were sent
To a Harvard dream in the Orient,
And some were held back safe in college towns
To love left wives of second lieutenants
Or speeding hippie chicks who shared their rents,
Wore muslin shifts . . . *frail painted cheeks like clowns.*

Urges linger like tipsy guests. Divorce and worse
Line up behind a tardy psychedelic hearse.

No Lady of Shallot

Back in the 60s (not yet THE SIXTIES),
Near lightning and stumbling thunder
Had emptied the links and pool at Twin Hills.

And a girl, hair wet, in new jeans, weejuns,
At the window of a stone house
Edged tight on the very far east of town

Watched as the long drought came roaring apart
With wind and horizontal rain
That humbled oaks, set old shingles clapping,

Turned the dry spruce free of its fibrous roots,
Quite unmindful of the low wall
Designed to keep ditch and world at yard's length.

Her pupils rounded wide to take it in.
An awful glee razzed up her spine
As mind danced in the throbbing disorder.

No Lady of Shallot, she looked, foresaw
The greater shakiness to come:
Ruined Camelot—long war—shamed Presidents.

(Not quite literally, of course. But still
The next decade failed to surprise:
The slow replay of a quick fast-forward.)

There is a certain virgin turn of soul
That defines the girl from woman.
She watched at the recessed Tudor window

Back in the 60s (not yet THE SIXTIES),
The day lightning and bum-thunder
Sent her home from the high pool at Twin Hills.

Preventive Grace

They never wed, so never quite divorced,
But just now met by canny happenstance
On the declining square (brickwork noon-scorched—
And scarcely June), contrived a gimpy dance,
Parleyed an inane word or two, and smiled
Toward the middle-distance. Once stung, twice wise,
Long immunized against what will beguile
Teens' buzzing surge, each copped a neutered guise
That would (but didn't) hide the plot devised
Full forty years ago against a child
Who wasn't there—or let go on its own:
Some spotty blood, no discernible bone.

Abortions

After the first, Kate dreamed quite frequently
That a gutted kitten, eyeless and gray,
Revolved on a cracked lazy-susan's tray
And mewed from hunger. It had no belly.

The dream dispersed with the shifting weather.
She met Mark at a Green Party rally.
On her laptop, she'd playfully tally
Their double comings. He favored leather.

She missed one period, then two. Then Mark
Missed Pam and his boys. Kate had another
(At his expense), moved back with her mother
In Lowell, and took to jogging after dark.

Every now and then, in the office, gym, or mall,
She strains to hear a blinded kitten's empty call.

Monsters

Some kids are unready for mainstreaming,
Not well-equipped. I don't mean Antoinette,
Who was by then all she'd become, straining
At her gnawn-self. Her feral glare begged *Let
Me Be*, so we didn't. Our savagery
Proved us normal, and in that we rejoiced.

Years late, this necromantic memory:
 *Watch, her hisses spray; hall-monitors gasp,
 but look away; stunned mercy goes unvoiced,
 and we laugh while her rage growls, wails, and rasps.*

No, we were unready. Still are, it seems,
Ready to trawl for sports in the deep womb:
Webbed hands, nubbed-brain, propensity for gloom—
Coded errors confute our fastidious dreams.

Lilith

Because her name is liquid on our Northern tongue
And rolls slow as cloved oil or honeyed cream,
We forget what Adam came to know: Dung
Dried to her lean haunches, her voice the scream
Of stubby chalk against ungiving slate.

We tramp a wet, awakened dream. Now she can wait
Apart from caves and lunar groves and stare
As a stunned, fey child from a slick cover.
Clack at the *net*? She vends your fetish there,
Queen of page and screen, our demon lover.

Since now Lilith, ageless, has lately come of age,
And raptors children in her taloned rage,
Best be content with Eve, the flawed mother
Of all who live, forsaking that Other
Who is older than Eden, plumed, and rank
As Moloch's hole, where Being fades to blank.

Baton Rouge

3/9/70

She reads and smokes with rapt intensity,
Free of haste or affectation, like some
Men handle a shovel naturally,
Each motion economical, outcome
Maximized, working her strong lungs and heart
Together at a scarcely heightened pace.
In his old pink oxford shirt, she seems part
Boy, hunched shoulders, no hips. Her breasts and face
Refute that notion. A stiff bandanna
Brings her eyes and mouth to a bold relief,
Hides her fine hair, and is gathered in a
Small tight knot behind her neck. For a brief
Moment, he thinks how, surprised, she'd cry out
If he twisted it. They'd argue. He'd shout.
They might reconcile and make love slow, hard.
Out back, the neighbor woman sweeps her yard;
Her son left Wednesday, banging the screen door.
Nor is this room Eden, clapboard wainscot and cypress floor.

In the Maze at Mandeville

(a story told for true long after the fact)

Crazed, in the gray-walled maze called Mandeville,
You came true and to yourself, suddenly,
On a Tuesday in May at a quarter-to-three.

And reclamation, like an orgasm, rolled,
Till you shivered and almost laughed outright.
You stood, but stopped your throat, uptight.

You can't let yourself go (whenever you're ready)
From (and in) the maze at Mandeville,
Where sanity's scarce: "You're quite unsteady . . . ."

Ward-wisdom points to fat black Bess,
Whose sound importunings were taken for stress.

after shock: death-mask with afro-glow

She's there for the duration.
But not you, you fox.
You packaged yourself in a neat little box.

You thanked the staff when they were down;
Let them suggest the first trip into town;
Moved comely and clean in your starchy white gown.

You had not meant
To spend so much time with Baptists
In the basement.

But it worked.

And those who had put you there (in an altogether
        complex sense)
Came to take you home. The long ride north was quiet
        and tense.
Abiding and sharp as the proverbial tack,
You determined then they'd not get you back.
They won't, as long as you recall

The world is Mandeville since the Fall:
To shake off the hard, sustaining yoke
Is to bare your nape beneath the stroke.

The Turning Year

The whirl of autumn birds
Careens, then thins, thickens,
Finds its prefigured place
And settles to itself:

Shadowed and shadow one dim stain on pasture grass.

This time last year, she watched
While a starling'd ribbon
As black as hangman's silk
Unwound its blind angle
Against the clouding west:

From Okarche toward Moore,
Miles of south-seeking birds whose purpose she wanted.

Lady, before last light, turn home.

There supper must be made
And homework signed. Then you
Might listen to Old Brahms,
Who'll make the speakers bulge
With taut, declining strings
And sad, low liquid brass.

A whirl of autumn birds sinks to its shadow on the grass.

Father to Son

You will find, boy, that more than one grown man
Carries with him a memory buried
Deep in his loins like a pellet. It can
Give him no grief for years, then he's harried
Three nights running in his safe married bed.
Because he can't recall a face quite right
Or remember words that were left unsaid,
A leaden ache draws his cold scrotum tight.

Is what wakens him a kink in the brain?
A wrinkled record out of displaced time?
The gnawing of a perennial crime?
Or a simple response to thunder? Rain?

Or none of these? To be a man may mean blank grief
Jerks you erect, with a dull wound and no relief.

Call and Response

i.

What we did to old lovers will suffice,
But the stray deed once left undone is what
Might ruin us yet, decades later, that nice,
Displaced mercy: the painted board's dry-rot.

Why not historicize? Her surrender,
Duly prescribed, derived from Sexton's verse
And faux-folk tunes. Acts she's unremember,
But can't, slick-shifted bliss into reverse.

He played things cool and kinky, came and went.
[*Slow fade to black*] Returning now and then,
He kept her bound (tall, straight, but strangely bent).
By June he neither called nor came again.

How then to make deferred restitution
For a less than honest prostitution?

ii.

Your straggler's conscience is self-indulgence,
An old endearing fault. You beg pardon
For things you think I'd best unremember,
But won't: That Vera scarf; my ditzy tears.

You got me started. Say that and be still.
It was a time to try on men. I did.
Your friend Benson was quick compensation,
No real comfort, a viscous interlude;
But that married black boy did much better,
Took his sweet time (no hectic churning there),
Until I caught enough from him to guess
What I might claim and husbands had to give.

I like my work and love my unprecocious Tim:
You turned me loose so I could find a man, like him.

Two Ancient Lyrics

I

Sing, sluttish Persephone,
　　a round of spring run sour . . .

　　　　with amber days like knotted gauze
　　　　when the streets themselves give up their dead
　　　　as vapors out of gutter grates
　　　　blackening the cracks along the curb
　　　　to where the children chalk out hopscotch squares.

Beside the sidewalk,
　　the rain leaves puddles for worms to drown in,
　　drizzling by way of crocodile tears.

II

Dark dreams of a darker sleep,
　　　　where old gods grope on tangled tongues
　　　　through litanies lost within the lines
　　　　of three abandoned books.

gray mold grows on these abandoned books

In subearthen summer night,
　　　　down the stony cellar steps . . .

　　　　Don't read the faded labels wrong
　　　　that warn you not to crawl along
　　　　the cracks in old concrete.

Passion Sunday

From East to West . . . and every parish church
Anew Jerusalem, our hosannas
Ringing to the arcing sway of censers
We wave the green and pointed shafts of palm
Like swords. Are we eager of Malchus' ear?

Perhaps.

So think ahead.
Less than a week and these new strips of palm
Will flake like rough-forged nails, assume an edge
Like a lance-point.

Recall how the ashes of last year's palms
Marked us for this season's lunge toward Grace.

Adoration at 2 a.m.

Only a layman, you have your practiced
Ritual nonetheless. Wife and daughters
Asleep, you try to nap, or channel-surf
For innocent reruns, then shower, shave,
Dress, read something (perhaps) appropriate,
And drive into the early morning night.

You follow these streets in every season:
Through lightning and blown rain in troubled spring,
Or humid blackness of still midsummer;
Under drifting moons of sudden autumn,
Or clear, far stars that make the winter sky.
The trip itself is a step out of time.

At journey's end, a stranger like you will
Surrender his vigil. You take his place
Before the monstrance filled with What we seek
And repray old promises for an hour.

Back home again, you dream briefly toward dawn.

Two Refugees

The pews of early Mass: and once again
I recognize at once the common face.
The wrinkles radiate from mouth and chin
And eyes, a fragile yet a lasting lace.
Outside Khe Sanh she ran. Her burden bent
Her forward with its weight, *la lune*-faced child
And bamboo bed, or at My Lai she went
Into the ditch that caught those bodies piled
Pell mell. But then we last assessed our fees
While Christmas bells were blasted in a rush
To ring in peace with power. The little priest
Lifts high the circling Host. The shufflers hush.
And so there waits for us this rockbound hope
Left still within the bombers' well-strewn trope.

My Father's Ankle

Only six, but playing Pershing
Under the porch on Tucker Street,
He disinterred a muddy shard
Of Mason jar and felt the sting
Leap up his calf. Out in the yard
The others stopped the game, discreet
In their surprised complicity.

The purpling flap betrayed the bone,
So Jeff had Nellie ring old Doc,
Who laced the place, said *Wait and see.*
An open shoe and cotton sock
Through rainy weeks 'til he was grown:
All boys were stoics in Shawnee;
He kept his silence, went to war.

Still a private, he made MP.
Then the damp fall of '42
Renewed the ache, deep-swollen, sore.
Discharged, distraught, he crossed the sea
To weld at Pearl, its water blue
As veins between the clouds and shore.
He'd dance late, drinking down the hurt.

In the dry-docked Pacific dawn,
He'd squat to the cruiser's bent hull
And file away new rust, some dirt
Or sand, then strike his arc, the dull
Regretful slag of last night gone.
Sparks that could blind peppered his shirt—
His hood in place, his cap turned back.

These things arrive at second hand:
Partial reports, nothing exact.
But I remember his rough, tanned
Neck, scarred lunch pail, and hurried track
Across the lawn, leaving for work . . .
His mind on miles of pipe, the land
Agleam with rain, his ankle's sudden jerk.

An Okie Parable

Dad showed me the ant-lion once
    in his inverted cone
In the fine caliche'd August dust
    (the floor of Grandad's shed),
Where hard bright spots of late-day light
    broke through a ragged board.

Watch and be still, he said; we crouched.
    Pop took a pinch of sand,
And fed it grain by silver grain
    into that funnel-spout.
A new cone formed; it pointed up . . .
    but not for very long.

A micro-fiend with nightmare jaws
    emerged and went berserk,
And hurled the sand with mitey force
    outside his tidy pit.
His fury spent, he nestled back
    and disappeared from sight.

Suppose an ant had lost his grip
    and come to rest down there.
The sides are steep, too loose to climb.
    There's hardly time to try.
The doodle-bug is quick and sure.
    He's hungrier than you.

I think you've learned a lesson, Son,
    my Daddy said to me:
Deep down in life are lurking things
    you hope to never see.

The Bicentennial Summer of '76

When the young doctor saw Pop's biopsy
Report and condescended to Mother
Outside the room, she suddenly could see
How it was people killed one another
From rage, for she grew murder in her heart
But let him live. He had the healing art
(Or so we thought). By the enabling light
Above our dining table, Dad and I
Sat late on more than one moth-ridden night
And patiently contrived how not to die.

> *Retire in six months, and build at the lake;*
> *A loft with half-bath for my sister's sake;*
> *A broad tiered deck; mantle of native stone;*
> *Good drainage; wood shingles; low-interest loan.*

He hummed to the blueprints a mantra, Hope,
And moved toward the dark up a greening slope.

The New Widow's Aubade

Something in the attic makes itself known
With flurried rasps—a squirrel half-grown
Or Norway rat; downstairs our cat patrols
The den and moans; the hall clock tolls
Some quarter-hour; the fridge kicks in and hums
Anew (louder). Though spongy crumbs
Of Hansel-Gretel dreams resist first light,
Again I've made it through the night.

Now coffee's on, half-dressed you search the yard
For *Morning News* (one must look hard
In unmown grass), then leave the paper wrapped.
That squirrel or rat will go untrapped.

The Passing

(In memory of Charles Gordone, the first playwright of African descent to win the Pulitzer Prize, 1970)

No use to conjure eyes'
Locked stare—though clear of every mote
And much less beam, nor cries
Of rooks that cough a single note.

Much rather hear the jing
And wrangle of quicksilver spurs,
While Buck and Rooster sing
Of Adam's chill and gritty curse.

Along the patient breaks
Of the wind-keened Canadian,
A cedar-shadow quakes;
December settles on the land.

Your dark and angry art
Grew out of our divided fate
And your inclusive heart.
You hurt beyond the pull of hate.

The play will live, of course.
You learned to move without applause,
Derived a western source,
And ran to earth the Primal Cause.

The Cemetery: Carney OK

i.

Toward the far back, by the greening Cyclone-gate,
    where the headstones' reach has years to come,
    an independent has cased his well.

His woodpecker pump dips and plocks.

It dips and plocks its statutory way across these prairie seasons,
    nodding out a regulated time that disdains
    vernal dewlight and noisy August noons,
    near autumn moons, and February rains,
But is measured and ledgered somewhere.

ii.

These graves look east,
    but began when a wagon headed south
    lost twin boys the same day.

They cast knobby slabs in thin cement,
    knifed in names, then dates, then creaked away.

(Who added this greasy coat of silver paint that blisters,
    peels, and flakes?)

iii.

Once the town came, a steady dying fed the ground:

    Influenza, another war, and more,
    but mostly the old and born-too-soon,
    careening drunks from Tryon who missed the bridge,
    and the new Buick that tried to pass
    as a tank-trunk cleared the cedar-ridge.

iv.

They buried out of homes at first, and in a hurry:

> Picks cracked the crusted earth,
> shovels caked with red clay squared the stubborn hole.
> Bonham-Walker in Chandler soon assumed the role,
> and the county provides a backhoe now.

It chugs aside,
> shuts down until the family goes.

v.

The old town curls like a fossil snail,
> a calcite husk, a bent, corroded nail:

> John's drugstore with its stone cellar and torn
> > screen-doors;
> Opal's haunted grocery's warped linoleum floors.

The broken doughboy in the neglected park
> has pitted rods for ankle-bones
> and lends his shadow toward the dark.

coda

What little life is left straddles the highway now.
A Circle-K glares down the Lonesome Rancher Grill.
Rent-a-Video stocks lewd laughs and thrills,
While the woodpecker pump lifts, plocks, and bows.

Scaling Parnassus

i. *Hybris*

> Rachmaninoff
> Strains, disdains, these small tight hands:
> Dropped notes, broken chords.

ii. Practice, practice, practice

> Tantalizing phrase,
> Perfect, as if wrought by God:
> Yet fingers fumble.

iii. Legato

> Pedal if you must:
> Best to shift the fourth finger
> To the depressed key.

iv. *Realpolitik*

> Weak hand, take the lead
> In those sudden doubled-thirds:
> Slower, but certain.

v. What Mr. Ricker Said

> Play into the keys.
> Preconceive the sound you'd make
> When the hammer lifts.

Driving East after Rita

Last chance for gas west of Beaumont,
    four tired state troopers mind the cue—
    no panic here, a strict cortege.

The Pac-N-Go suggests Kirkut,
    but this Exxon was scarcely grazed—
    some tumbled signs, wind-dropped debris.

Force-fed at last onto I-10,
    what cars we meet are left unclaimed—
    the low tight sky devoid of birds.

Alone we cruise above the town,
    all exits closed, live-oaks upturned—
    small houses once again unframed.

Downed lines define new neighborhoods
    patrolled by packs of blank-faced dogs—
    dull wink of glass in dead graylight.

Now this once-ordered world stands out
    for what it is and always was—
    ungrateful, quantum-haunted space.

"Katrina refugees return—weigh future"

The photo, widely syndicated, shows
A woman and son, their midcity home
Awash in sludge, intent on saving some
Long boxy thing. A teak armoire? Who knows?

It's Chan for sure (you can and do see that),
No matronly *maman* you're pleased to say,
Bird-boned and delicate as on the day
She split—and bruised your mind, but fed the cat.

Decades ago, you wished her ill, and yet
Had hardly asked for this: Those gulag eyes
Have left off questioning. Beyond surprise
She does what hands can do, takes what she'll get.

If curses work, then benediction stands a chance:
Dread Lord, bless mother, son, and all new mendicants.

The Franciscan Martyrs: New Mexico, 10 August 1680

i.

High coyote yelp at moonset
And owl-murmur—
Dawn of San Lorenzo's Day.

Fray Juan Baustista Pío
Broke the night's fast with goat's milk
And left the *convento* in Santa Fe.

His turn at Holy Mass in Tesuque.

At the last steep turn
He reined the pied mule
Hard right at the puddled wall,

Where a brazen lizard
Glared back his glance;
Hay, hermano diablo, he said and laughed.

The pueblo wholly unpeopled,
Blank with mid-morning sun,
The friar followed a dog's bark

Into the near ravine,
A dry, shrubby *riíto*-bed
Churning with silence.

One of the baptized women screamed.

Then it was a short lance,
Iron-tipped for bear or elk,
Snapped under his chin,

And cinched his jaws,
Lifted his weathered tonsure,
But failed to break it.

His lay companion
Scurried the news to Santa Fe,
That day of dread—San Lorenzo's Day.

ii.

Given the spare chronicles, such a re-creation,
Based on what few details we think we know,
Carries no disrespect, may in fact show
A certain praiseworthy identification
With martyrdom that benefits the soul—
A pious fiction with truth as its goal.

iii.

This little we do know, names and places:

> At Galisteo, two, Fathers Juan Bernal and
>   Domingo de Vera;
> At windy Pecos on plains-edge, Fernando de
>   Velasco (30 yrs a missioner);
> In Nambé, Tomás de Torres, of Tepozotlán;
> At San Ildefonso, two, Luis de Morales and
>   Brother Antonio Sánches de Pro — "who from
>   the Descalces passed to the Observancia";
> In Picurís, Padre Matías Rendón;
> Two more in high Taos, Antonio de Mora and
>   Brother Juan de la Pedosa;
> On the Turquoise Trail at San Marcos, Fray
>   Manuel Tinoco;
> In Santo Domingo, three, Padres Francisco
>   Antonio de Lorenzana, Juan de Talabán
>   *(custodio habitual)*, and Joseph de Montesdoca;
> At Jemez, Padre Juan de Jesús, far from Granada;
> On Acoma, near the sun, Lucas Maldonado
>   *(definidor actual)*;
> At Alona, the Castilian, Fray Juan de Bal.

As the sun moved west,

> At lost Xongopavi, Padre Joseph de Truxillo, of

>>> storied virtues;
>> In Aguatubi, Fray Joseph de Figueroa;
>> At old Oraibi, Joseph de Espeleta (30 yrs a
>>> missioner) and Agustín de Santa María.

Where possible and with sufficient warning,
They no doubt consumed the Host,
Thus sparing assassins a greater sin.

iv.

Another day will come,
At once vacuous and rabid,
When the charge-card shall reign.

Reconquered Santa Fe
Is dispossessed again.

>> Franciscan zeal for souls,
>> Baptism and sweet oil of chrism:
>> *"Tools of rank imperialism!"*

New Age pimps the kivas—
Discounted kachinas.

It is late in the day.

v.

If you're like me, "a pilgrim sore bereft,"
Follow the Paseo de Peralta
(Though old Don Pedro was no friend of friars)
And climb the steep little hill to the left.

The most reliable guidebooks agree
That the view from the Cross of the Martyrs
At sunset repays a tourist's efforts,
But what you seek is more than you will see.
Recite the names and places, try to pray
Like the child you were and still hope to be.
Do not presume to warrant martyrdom,
But prime yourself for San Lorenzo's Day.

2495 Redding Road

It takes some time to raise a barn or two:
The tardy glacier plants its hoarded stones
Reluctantly, and timid woods push north
One season at a time—retreat, regroup,
And harden toward the beams they will become
Once Yankee pluck and cagey faith arrive
With bar and adze to make the most of what's
At hand. Unsanded planks embrace the peg
And corner-notch, confound Atlantic gales
That leap the Sound to be at ox and man.
Spring thaw, like sleet, tries stone and timberwork
Alike for well one-hundred years and more.

Fairfield indeed, though farmers drop their bones,
Small land-holds merge, new peoples are declared,
Then tear apart and reunite, renewed.
The not-so-placid 1950s come:
A Southern man and Yankee bride take charge.
Derive upon those stones and old-growth wood
A place of sturdy grace, turn out their books,
Raise up their get, eat well, drink long with friends,
Invest a home with royalties and sweat
(The latter most exactingly applied),
Then shed their bones in turn, but in an age
When reclamations fail to fetch the price.

Location's where it's at, so build anew.
It takes no time to raze a barn or two.

After Thirty Years: An Anniversary Poem

Week's end: browning our penitential trout,
My wife hums and weaves to "The Sloop John B."
In tripping back the past, what does she see?
Which boys? What beach? I take the chilled wine out,
Return her smile. Marriage is mystery
(*Sacramentum*); to not know is not doubt.

It is, rather, to wonder: Not about
What was or might be yet—quick jealousy
That mimics love, reducing *we* to *me*.
No, we'd reclaim an old, neglected route
In a shrill fog where needles disagree
On what's true north, nations rage, vegans pout,

For One Unseen has wrapped his bleeding hands with ours
And tugs us past dim principalities and powers.

Humanae Vitae

Entangled in the heedless arms and legs of love,
     lovers do not lose time
     (the tool that hollows skulls),
But set it tripping syncopate
To beat of bodies hard with heated certainty.

     They strain for Eden, where a fountain rose.

Encircled in its shrinking amniotic sea,
     the little heart makes time
     (the tool that chisels minds),
In keeping with a metronome
That drums above with cordial regularity.

     They strain for Eden, where a fountain rose.

Enraptured by the hungry tug at nipple's end,
     she claims this plenal time
     (the tool that fastens ties),
Then looks toward windows leaking day
And knows how action yields potentiality.

coda

old ways are best, from east to west;
love's sudden strife engenders life,

that strains for Eden, where a fountain rose.